Disclaimer

D1745376

The ideas, concepts, and opinions expressed in this book are intended for educational purposes only. This book is provided with the understanding the author is not rendering veterinary advice of any kind, nor is this book intended to provide veterinary advice, nor to diagnose, prescribe, or treat any disease or condition. No information in this book can take the place of the advice of a licensed veterinarian or poultry nutritionist. You are responsible for your own judgment and decisions.

Love this book and want even more backyard chicken goodness?

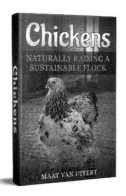

Itching to start your own backyard chicken flock....but totally scared you'll mess it up?

Grab my book, "Chickens: Naturally Raising A Sustainable Flock" and get started on the right foot - with information you can trust.

Brought to you by backyard chicken expert, Maat van Uitert, "Chickens: Naturally Raising A Sustainable Flock" is a 150-page ebook that guides you through every aspect of backyard chicken ownership.

This full-color, gorgeous Amazon Best Seller ebook contains over 40 behind-the-scenes photos and simple to follow recipes to keep your hens healthy....and laying fresh, delicious eggs.

Available on Amazon or on my website. Go to https://thefrugalchicken.com/CNRASF to save 10% off the list price.

Printed in the United States of America

First Printing, 2017

ISBN 978-1983483387

Stoney Ledge Publishing
123 Main Street
Clarkton, MO 63837

www.StoneyLedgePublishing.com

About The Author

Maat van Uitert (pronounced May-aht van Eye-tert) is an author, blogger, and founder of Pampered Chicken Mama, which reaches 10 million readers every month across social media. She's the author of 2 best selling Amazon books, Organic By Choice: The (Secret) Rebel's Guide To Backyard Gardening and Chickens: Naturally Raising A Sustainable Flock. Maat has been featured on NBC, CBS, ABC, and in Glamour, Prevention, Reader's Digest, and Women's Health. Maat lives on a 10 acre homestead in Southeast Missouri with her husband and two children.

Contents

Cluck Cakes™

Cream Cheese & Honey
Frosting

How To Make Cream Cheese

Cayenne Peas & Mealworm
"Chex Mix"

Sunflower, Peanut, & Black
Soldier Fly Larvae "Granola"

Coconut oil, Parsley, & Black
Soldier Fly Larvae Treats

How to Get The Most From This Book

Making treats for your chickens is one of the best parts of chicken ownership. You get to express yourself creatively and share a fun, bonding experience with your flock at the same time. Just remember that while this book is a fun cookbook to help you create delicious treats for backyard chickens, it's not a replacement for a well-rounded and balanced diet for your hens.

When creating your own treats, you can use these recipes in their entirety or make substitutions as the season or your pantry contents allow. These recipes are meant to be a framework; the real fun comes from adding your own special touches to your culinary creations that are special to you and your chickens.

Below are lists of swaps, options, and background information about the different components of each recipe. Think of these lists a little like a Chinese food take out menu—take a little from column A, substitute with column B, etc. The lists aren't all-inclusive, and if there's a particular ingredient your hens love that doesn't appear below, feel free to include it in your creations anyway. The most important thing is you have fun!

Protein options

Mealworms
Black soldier fly lar-
vae
Grubs
Crickets
Freshwater shrimp
Peanuts or other nuts
(unsalted with no
added flavors only!)

Herb options

Calendula
Oregano
Sage
Parsley
Lavender
Rosemary
Tarragon
Marjoram
Turmeric

Fat options

Coconut oil
Bacon grease
Lard
Tallow
Herb-infused olive oil

Seed options

Sunflower
Flax
Chia

Notes

Try to use USA-sourced insects. Insects sourced overseas are often fed questionable ingredients with little thought for the end user.

There's many small businesses out there that cater to backyard chicken owners and that use sustainable practices to raise their insects humanely.

You can buy herbs on Amazon, but if you want to grow them yourself, it's easy and preferable since you know they've not been exposed to any weed killers or other toxins.

For more information...

In my book Herbs In Your Backyard: 30 Herbs You Can Grow (Backyard Chicken Edition), I show you how to grow each of these herbs.

For more information, go to https://thefrugalchicken.com/HIMBY **

Feeding Backyard Chickens

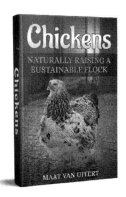

*** This chapter is an excerpt from my book Chickens: Naturally Raising A Sustainable Flock. If you want an easy, fun, down-to-earth manual for raising hens that you can turn to time and again, you can buy Chickens: Naturally Raising A Sustainable Flock from me or on Amazon.

If you want to buy directly from me (10% off plus a free digital version) go to https://thefrugalchicken.com/CNRASF. Enjoy! ***

Feeding backyard chickens

Feeding your chickens the best diet possible is the most important thing you'll do for them as their owner, and the quality of their eggs and meat depends on the quality of their food.

Through diet, you can not only provide beneficial nutrients to your flock, but by using all-natural supplements, you can reduce pathogens, improve gut health, increase nutrient absorption, and combat infection.

Necessary equipment

To successfully raise chickens, there's some necessary equipment they will need, namely, waterers, feeders, and a brooder. Anything that holds water and food and can be cleaned easily will suffice, but I recommend purchasing equipment specifically designed for poultry. Chicks in particular can fall into waterers and drown, and they do so quite easily.

If you have a number of chicks, getting a plastic or galvanized steel feeder is your best option. The longer feeders can meet the needs of several chicks. Chicks under 12 weeks old should have food available 24 hours a day, and the longer feeders mean you have to fill it less.

When chicks reach 12 weeks of age, they do not need feed around the clock, but I suggest purchasing a second feeder to make sure every bird has a shot at eating, depending on how many chicks you have. Many times owners don't add equipment as chicks grow older, only to find that their feathered friends haven't gotten enough to eat and are now sick.

When it comes to waterers for chicks, I suggest purchasing a mason jar waterer, which will allow you to use a mason jar to hold the water. These are advantageous because you can easily clean and swap out a mason jar, and the waterers are relatively inexpensive. They are also shallow, making it difficult for newborn chicks to fall in.

A plastic one is better than a metal one because in the winter, the plastic is less likely to freeze, and in my experience, the plastic ones are easier to wash. However, both are perfectly acceptable.

If possible, I recommend suspending the waterer above the ground. Chicks are messy, and very quickly will block their waterer with shavings, food, or feces, and you'll spend the better part of your day cleaning them out.

While suspending the waterer won't entirely prevent them from jamming up the waterer with debris, it does help. As the chicks get older, you will have to add waterers to their brooder, otherwise you might find yourself refilling it several times a day.

Feeding chickens from chicks to layers

Your chickens' dietary requirements change as they get older. Newborn chicks, growing pullets, and young roosters have specific dietary needs. If they're not met, your chickens might not grow well or become unhealthy.

Chicks (newborn to 12 weeks)

For chicks, I give them an 18 percent protein commercial chick starter to eat until they're 12 weeks old. Whether you feed medicated or non-medicated starter is up to you.

So what's the difference between non-medicated and medicated feed? Medicated feed contains a medication that helps chicks build an immunity to parasites naturally found in the environment. These parasites are one of the top killers of baby chicks, and they like moist environments. Medicated chick start is one way to help prevent them from infesting your chickens, and a second way is to keep their environment very clean and as free of moisture as possible.

The thing about medicated chick feed is it only helps chicks build an immunity if they're actually exposed to the parasites. The easiest way to do this is to either allow your chicks to go outside for a period of time during the day (in a tractor, for example) or to toss some dirt in their brooder if you're raising them inside.

Young pullets/roosters (12 weeks until they lay)

Young pullets and roosters should eat a grower feed that contains between 16 percent and 18 percent protein. Most commercial grower rations out there contain 16 percent protein. When it comes to a grower feed, it's very important to only use a feed that's labeled as a starter/grower ration (it might also just be called a grower feed).

Layer feed also usually contains 16 protein, so it's easy to substitute one for the other, but layer feed has extra calcium in it to support hens that lay eggs. This extra calcium can easily wreak havoc on the systems of a growing chick, damaging its organs. Kidneys, for example, are particularly vulnerable.

Pullets and young roosters should eat a grower ration until the pullets start laying, or the roosters turn about 26 weeks old. It's perfectly fine to allow your growing chickens to free range during this time.

Layers

Once they begin to lay, offer your hens a layer feed, which usually contains 16 percent protein, but you can also feed a game bird feed that's 22 percent protein.

Every flock is different, and even every chicken is different. I've personally had some chickens that do well on a 16 percent protein feed, but then I've had others that require a 22 percent game feed in order to lay regularly.

My advice is to start with a 16 percent layer ration, and increase the protein if you find they're not laying well. If you don't want to feed a 22 percent pellet, you can simply offer more protein in the form of mealworms (fresh or freeze dried) or something else to increase their protein.

Once hens start laying, they will need an extra calcium supplement, such as oyster shells or eggshells to ensure they produce good, hard eggs. Offer this in a separate dish, not mixed with the feed. Personally, I avoid giving them egg shells, but that's a choice individual to my flock. One of my hens realized she could eat her own eggs to get the shells she loves so much, but eggshells are another great source of calcium.

I highly suggest not bothering with scratch. It doesn't contain the necessary amount of protein, and for the money, you could easily purchase an additional bag of feed. There's not enough vitamins in it to justify the expense.

Feeding a flock of different ages

If you have to feed layers and chicks together, you're better off sticking to an 18 percent non-medicated grower ration and supplementing with oyster shells for your layers.

Your chicks will get the proper amount of protein they need to grow while the hens will get the extra calcium they need from the oyster shells. While there's some chance the chicks will pick up a piece of oyster shell here or there, the chicks are unlikely to consume a lot of it.

For more information...

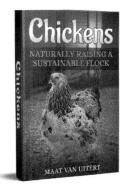

*** This prior chapter was an excerpt from my book Chickens: Naturally Raising A Sustainable Flock.

If you want an easy, fun, down-to-earth manual for raising hens that you can turn to time and again, you can buy Chickens: Naturally Raising A Sustainable Flock from me or on Amazon.

If you want to buy directly from me (10% off plus the digital version for free) go to https://thefrugalchicken.com/CNRASF. ***

Organic Homemade Chicken Feed Recipe

Ingredients

Sprouted seeds (5 cups)
Peas (2.5 cups)
Oats (2.5 cups)
Sunflower seeds (2 tablespoons)
Mealworms (1/2 cup)

Directions

Mix together just prior to feeding your hens. Feeds 5 chickens. While this homemade recipe usually works well, you might need to scale up or down a bit depending on your flock's needs, and whether you allow them to forage. This recipe easily doubles and triples.

Notes

I leave corn out of my homemade recipes, although adding a handful to your chicken's dinner during the coldest days of winter will do some good since they'll need an additional source of energy to help them stay warm.

Although corn is a great source of energy, it's really nothing but empty calories for chickens. It's included in many chicken feeds because it's a cheap filler that manufacturers use to extend the ingredients that provide actual value.

Can you raise a chicken on corn successfully? Yes.And there's plenty of people who do it. But corn is around 9 percent protein, and in my area, you can buy it for about $7 for a 50-pound bag. For just a dollar more, I can buy a decent commercial layer feed or a 50-pound bag of wheat berries that I can grow into fodder both are much better for your chickens than corn.

Wheat, peas, and mealworms (both live and freeze dried) are an excellent source of protein that hens love, while the oats are an excellent source of fiber in a homemade recipe. The sesame and sunflower seeds are great for fat, and the sunflower seeds especially are full of nutrients.

Calendula, Chia Seed, & Black Soldier Fly Larvae Oatmeal Breakfast

Makes enough for 5 chickens

Ingredients

3 cups warm oatmeal prepared with whole milk
1 tablespoon chia seeds
1 tablespoon dried or fresh calendula
1/4 cup black soldier fly larvae, mealworms, or other dried insects
Rosemary, for garnish

Directions

To prepare the oatmeal, combine with milk until the oatmeal is just soaked. Combine all ingredients and serve to your hens as part of a complete diet.

Notes

You can use either quick oats or regular oats, as long as it's only oats (no additives, preservatives, or flavoring.) Whole milk or cream is best.

Summer: add fresh-squeezed orange juice and thyme to combat heat stress.

Winter: heat oatmeal and add corn for a late-night snack to keep your flock warm during chilly nights.

Pumpkin Flax Cluck Cookies™

Makes about 12 cookies
Serving size: 1 cookie per chicken

Ingredients

1 cup pumpkin
2 eggs
⅓ cup oil
2 cups organic whole wheat flour
½ cup ground flax
1 tsp baking soda
¼ cup whole flax seeds

Directions

Preheat oven 350 degrees. In a large bowl, mix all the wet in-gredients (eggs, pumpkin, oil) together. In a separate bowl, mix the flour, ground flax, and baking soda together.

Add the dry ingredients to the wet, combining until a uniform dough is formed and the flour is incorporated. Sprinkle flour on a countertop and roll out the dough.

Using a cookie cutter or glass mason jar, cut out the dough and place on a cookie sheet. Bake at 350 degrees for about 15 minutes. Cookies will be soft.

When out of the oven, brush cookies with melted coconut oil

and sprinkle the flax seeds over the cookies. If desired, you can also sprinkle the cookies with calendula flower petals before the coconut oil dries.

Notes

If you spread the dough too thin, you'll end up with a wafer type cookie, which can be difficult for beaks to pierce.

Leaving the dough a bit thicker - about ¼ inch - allows for a softer cookie, which is easier for your flock to enjoy. If you want, you can substitute bacon grease for the coconut oil. It forms a thicker layer, but chickens LOVE it.

Peanut, Sunflower Seed, & Oregano Breakfast Oatmeal

Makes enough for 5 hens

Ingredients

3 cups warm oatmeal prepared with water
1 tablespoon oregano (fresh or dried)
1/4 cup raw peanuts
1/4 cup raw sunflower seeds
1/4 cup black soldier fly larvae, mealworms, or other dried insects

Directions

Prepare oatmeal with warm water. If desired, you can use cold water with the oatmeal and microwave to soften the oats. Combine all ingredients in a bowl right before breakfast.

Notes

To ensure the oatmeal isn't too warm, make sure it's only slightly warm to your touch. I call this "toddler warm," because it's about how hot you'd prepare oatmeal for a toddler.

Be sure to only use raw, unsalted peanuts and sunflower seeds. Too much salt might cause electrolyte imbalances in your chickens Black soldier fly larvae provide protein, peanuts and sunflower seeds provide fat, and oregano helps with overall health and a healthy immune system.

Mint, Parsley, & Eggshell Herb Salad

Makes enough for 5 hens

Ingredients

1 cup kale
¼ cup calendula
¼ cup mint
Mint flowers, if available
¼ cup parsley
½ cup eggshells
2 tablespoons flax seeds

Directions

Combine all ingredients in a bowl and serve immediately.

Notes

You can use freeze dried or fresh kale. Often, freeze dried kale is more nutritious and easier for chickens to eat. Mint helps with digestive health, while calendula and kale have important nutrients. The eggshells offer calcium, an important mineral for strong eggshells.

Peanut Butter Honey Cluck Cakes™

Makes approximately 12 mini cupcakes or 6 normal-size cupcakes

Ingredients

¼ cup peanut butter
1 egg
1 cup organic whole wheat flour
¼ cup high-quality olive oil
⊠ cup honey
1 tsp baking soda
⊠ cup quick-start oats
Chia seeds & mint leaves and flowers (if available) for garnish

Directions

Preheat oven to 350 degrees. Combine wet ingredients (peanut butter, egg, oil, and honey) and dry ingredients (flour, baking soda, and oats) in separate bowls, then add the dry ingredients to the wet. Mix thoroughly until a dough is formed.

Spoon into a mini cupcake or a regular-sized cupcake pan. Bake at 350 degrees for 15 to 20 minutes, or until a toothpick inserted comes out clean. Frost with cream cheese frosting (see recipe) or bacon grease.

Notes

The mini cupcakes mean that more chickens can have a chance at a Cluck Cake if you have more than a few hens. The chia seeds make nice "sprinkles" while the dried mint leaves and flowers give something extra to peck at. Both are great for gut health. My chickens go straight for the leaves and mint flowers.

While your chickens shouldn't have too much peanut butter, the amount in this recipe, spread out over a lot of Cluck Cakes, is minimal. Only use all-natural peanut butter with no additives or sugars. If there's some salt in the peanut butter, it's fine. The danger comes from feeding them excessive amounts of salt or feeding salt day in and day out.

Cream Cheese & Honey Frosting

Ingredients

8 ounces full fat cream cheese with no preservatives or flavoring
1 tablespoon organic honey (optional)

Directions

Allow the cream cheese to soften at room temperature. This step is critical so your frosting comes out of the piping bag easily. When softened, combine with honey in a bowl. Use a piping bag to frost Cluck Cakes™ or Cluck Cookies™.

Notes

Try to find organic honey from a local beekeeper. You're supporting a local artisan and providing a higher quality honey for your flock. If the honey hasn't been strained, that's fine. Honey purchased at the grocery store might be more corn syrup than honey, and typically has been so filtered, most of the pollen has been removed. Manuka honey might add some extra health benefits.

You can also make your own cream cheese at home fairly easily, which ensures your chickens only eat organic food without preservatives or undisclosed ingredients.

How To Make
Cream Cheese

Ingredients

2 quarts cream
Mesophilic culture or cream cheese culture (either will work)

Directions

Heat the cream to 85 degrees F. When the right temperature, remove from heat and stir in culture. Use a slotted spoon in an up down motion to ensure it's completely mixed. Cover and allow to culture overnight.

The following morning, the culture will look like yogurt, and you'll see a whitish-yellow liquid (the whey). Put the cheese into a cheese cloth and strain until the whey has drained and the cheese is solid. Allow to firm up in the refrigerator.

(Cream cheese for human consumption includes salt. I've left it out of this recipe since your chickens shouldn't eat too much salt).

Cayenne Peas & Meal-worm "Chex Mix"

Serves 5 chickens

Ingredients

1 teaspoon cayenne pepper
1 teaspoon turmeric
1 teaspoon paprika
1 teaspoon calendula flower petals
1 cup freeze dried or dried split peas
½ cup sunflower seeds
2 cups mealworms or other dried insects

Directions

Combine all ingredients in a bowl & serve immediately.

Notes

Chickens find this recipe tasty and the spices might help de-worm your chickens. The spiciness causes worms to detach from your chickens' insides, and they're expelled when your hens poop.

Make sure you use unsalted sunflower seeds. Too much salt can mess up your flock's electrolyte balance. Freeze dried or dried peas are both fine; often freeze dried peas will have more nutrients since they're harvested at peak ripeness.

Sunflower, Peanut, & Black Soldier Fly Larvae "Granola"

Makes enough for 5 hens

Ingredients

1/4 cup kale (fresh or freeze dried)
1/2 cup raw sunflower seeds
1/2 cup raw peanuts
1/4 cup black soldier fly larvae, mealworms, or other dried insects
Calendula or other herb for garnish

Directions

Combine all ingredients and serve to your hens as part of a complete diet.

Notes

Black soldier fly larvae provide protein, kale has important nutrients and calcium for healthy eggs, and peanuts and sunflower seeds provide fat.

Make sure you use raw, unsalted peanuts and sunflower seeds. Too much salt can mess up your flock's electrolyte balance.

Coconut Oil, Parsley, & Black Soldier Fly Larvae Treats

Makes 12 treats
Serving size: 1 treat per chicken

Ingredients

1 cup melted coconut oil
1 tablespoon parsley (fresh or dried)
1 berry (any type) per hen
1 tablespoon flax seeds
1/4 cup black soldier fly larvae, mealworms, or other dried insects

Directions

Combine all dry ingredients except berries. Pour melted coconut oil into a mini cupcake pan. Mix in dry ingredients and top with a sliced berry. Refrigerate until solid.

Notes

Black soldier fly larvae provide protein, berries and parsley have important nutrients, coconut oil provides fat, and flax helps support healthy skin and feathers.

Love this book & want even more back-yard chicken goodness?

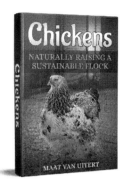

Itching to start your own backyard chicken flock....but totally scared you'll mess it up? Grab my book, "Chickens: Naturally Raising A Sustainable Flock" and get started on the right foot - with information you can trust.

Brought to you by backyard chicken expert, Maat van Uitert, "Chickens: Naturally Raising A Sustainable Flock" is a 150-page ebook that guides you through every aspect of backyard chicken ownership. This full-color, gorgeous Amazon Best Seller ebook contains over 40 behind-the-scenes photos and simple to follow recipes to keep your hens healthy....and laying fresh, delicious eggs.

Available on Amazon or on my website. Go to https://thefrugalchicken.com/CNRASF to save 10% off the list price.

More Books By Maat van Uitert

Chickens: Naturally Raising A Sustainable Flock

https://thefrugalchicken.com/CNRASF

Organic By Choice: The (Secret) Rebel's Guide To Backyard Gardening

https://thefrugalchicken.com/OBC

The Backyard Chicken Bundle

http://thebackyardchickenbundle.com

Hang Out With Me On Social Media!

 @thefrugalchicken

 @thefrugalchicken2

 @pamperedchickenmama

 https://thefrugalchicker.com/YouTube

PamperedChickenMama.com

Made in the USA
Monee, IL
15 November 2019